AuthorHouse™
1663 Liberty Drive
Bloomington, IN 47403
www.authorhouse.com
Phone: 1 (800) 839-8640

Published by AuthorHouse 03/07/2019

ISBN: 978-1-7283-0339-0 (sc)
ISBN: 978-1-7283-0338-3 (e)

Library of Congress Control Number: 2019902730

Print information available on the last page.

authorHOUSE®

# A Work Day the Firefighter Way

A Child's Rhyming Guide to Fire and Safety

## The Firefighter Writer

For my nieces
and nephews.

In this job of living the dream, you wouldn't believe the things I've seen.

I've seen houses a blaze and multiple fires, even wrecked cars from blown-out tires.

Before I get into the calls, let's start from the beginning and talk about firehouse living.

A firefighter starts in the morning because an emergency knows no time and can happen without warning.

Once at the station, the firefighter must check the rig. After all, a well-equipped truck is part of the gig.

He checks the pump and she checks the hose, then they both make sure the valves open and close.

The tank is full of water and the bottles full of air. Now to check and see if the tools are all there.

I see a shovel, an axe, and some foam in a jar. What is this strange tool? It must be a halligan bar.

The shovel is used with a lot of purpose but mainly to get trash off the ground surface.

A firefighter uses the axe to give walls and doors a whack!

We can fight fire from a gas leaking car with the foam from the jar.

The halligan bar opens doors for example but that is just a sample. It has multiple uses, with this tool there should be no excuses.

The exhaust fans are ready and so is the hydrant bag. Now to check the lights and the wig wag.

Exhaust fans are used to clear a room full of smoke, this is vital so no one will choke.

The hydrant bag is important on the truck, as it allows the firefighter to get water if the hydrant is stuck.

The wig wag is a flashing headlight, not to be confused with the siren which roars as loud as a lion!

The chainsaw has fuel, and the ladders are on the racks. Now for pike poles, masks, and hotel packs.

Chainsaws cut holes in roofs and clear roads from down trees, most fire departments have two different types of these.

Ladders extend to the top of the house, but heights can be scary like seeing a mouse.

Firefighters are brave so you don't have to be, I'm glad they are coming if they need to save me.

Pike poles are used to pull ceilings down to look in the attic and all around.

When going to a high-rise building with fire coming from its windows and stacks, we must get hose up there in bundles called hotel packs.

That is just some of the equipment we have and wanted to share, because of this, fire should beware.

The lights are shining bright, and the siren is working. Good thing the truck is ready, because somewhere a fire is lurking.

If there's a fire, what will I wear? It is now time to inspect my safety gear.

I have a coat and pants, a good helmet and hood. I also have boots and gloves to protect me from burning wood.

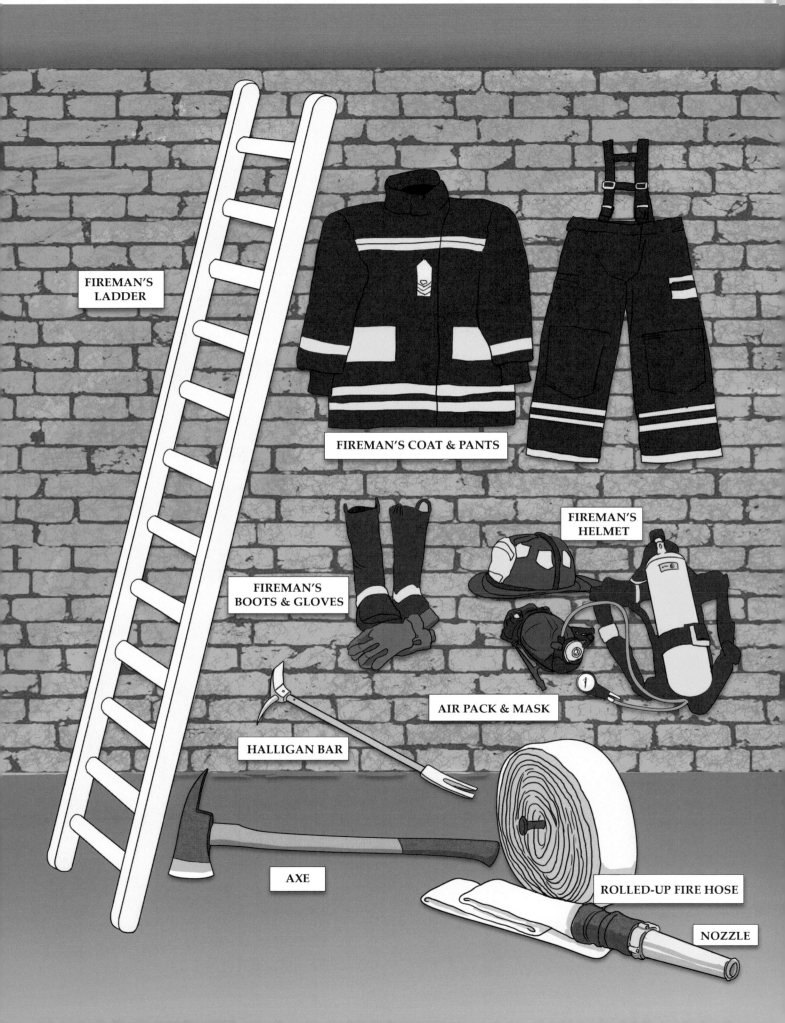

FIREMAN'S LADDER

FIREMAN'S COAT & PANTS

FIREMAN'S HELMET

FIREMAN'S BOOTS & GLOVES

AIR PACK & MASK

HALLIGAN BAR

AXE

ROLLED-UP FIRE HOSE

NOZZLE

Now we go inside to do our station duties, like taking out trash, sweeping and mopping, and making a list for our grocery shopping.

The fire station has rooms like a house: a bathroom, office, kitchen, and a room called the day. But we don't keep the trucks inside. They're kept in the bay.

You see, we live at the station for twenty-four hours a day, so we treat it like our house because it's where we stay.

We eat our meals at work, like breakfast, lunch, and dinner. If you're the new guy, you cook because you're the beginner.

The rookie provides humor around the fire station, like a character from a movie, a play, or animation.

In the firehouse, we have a Dalmatian named Daisy. Sometimes she's crazy, and sometimes she's lazy.

We can relax once we're ready for our shift, but if the bells ring we'd better move swift.

Training is important. It's how we prepare. And we often work with other departments and invite them to share.

Kids have fun when they visit the station; they treat it like a break from school, a recess, or vacation.

The object the kids from school often find most cool is our large brass fireman's pole.

It is important to keep it clean and shiny, because if we don't, the drop is not tiny.

Most of the day is spent training and improving. Uh oh! I just heard the bells. Time to get moving!

Let's make our way down the pole to the first floor, across the bay to the fire truck door.

Before we get in, we must put on our gear, but quietly listen. The radio has information for us to hear.

Speeding down the road, passing cars stopped on the right, we must slow down for traffic at a red light.

Firefighters are now preparing for the firefight; they sit in the back and put on their air packs.

As we arrive on scene, we see the flames get higher. We better grab the hose, because the house is on fire.

We grab the hose and the axe and head through the door. Time to be careful and make sure the fire hasn't burned through the floor.

We go through the house on our hands and our knees, all the while yelling, "If anyone's in here, answer me please!"

We make our way into the kitchen, under a table and chairs, down a narrow hallway, and then up the stairs.

We're still trying to help, yelling, "Is anyone here?" And in a bedroom, we see the fire is there.

We open the hose and knock the flames down. For it to stop, the fire must drown.

Just as we finish, we hear a boy named Fred. He cries out, "Please help me! I'm under the bed!"

We rescue Fred from under the bed, then help him outside. Luckily, he's okay, but he might go for an ambulance ride.

Nothing too serious, just to get checked out, but before he leaves, we tell him about getting out.

"Fred, when there's a fire, you must find an exit and make your way out. Then go to the neighbors and scream and shout."

"Yell, 'My house is on fire. Call 911! This isn't a joke! This isn't for fun!'"

Once you are out of the house that is where you stay. To prevent injury, you must keep away.

For you to go back in, it wouldn't be good. The fire department is for that. Let this be understood.

Remember you are a kid and shouldn't play with things that help a fire catch, like an oven, a candle, a lighter, or match.

If you are in a fire and clean air is your desire, then get low to the ground because the smoke is ceiling bound.

Stay low to the floor, and keep smoke out by putting a blanket under the door.

If you do catch on fire, do not panic. You must keep cool. Remember this lesson: stop, drop, and roll.

Most of all, in an emergency, don't be afraid to let out a yelp. Firefighters are your friends, and they are there to help.

So with all of that said–the fire extinguished
and Fred rescued from under the bed–

It is time to roll up the hoses and clean up
the fire grounds–and shut off the sirens
and pumps. We're done with the sounds.

Back to the station. Away we go. When is
our next fire? This we don't know.

We're back in the station. It is late now. Time to clean up and eat some chow.

After dinner, we are ready for our beds. We never sleep well with fires running through our heads.

It is now morning, time for us to go. The other firefighters will stay. We'll be back for our next shift; nothing can keep a good firefighter away.

Never forget what you have read. You can now save lives with what's in your head.

# About the Author

I grew up in northeast Ohio in a big family that always helped others in need through fostering children and various other endeavors. Because of this, I found my life passion of wanting to help people. I attended a local fire academy and Youngstown State University, where I majored in emergency medical technology, criminal justice, and allied health. During my time at YSU, I became certified as an EMT and paramedic and later earned a master's degree in health and human services. I have worked for over fifteen years as a firefighter, EMT, and paramedic. I continue to work as a career firefighter and paramedic for a professional fire department. In addition, I obtained a registered nurse's license and completed a bachelor's degree in nursing from Ohio University. Working as a nurse has also allowed me to grow as a health care provider. My hope is to reach children through this book and teach them about fire and safety in a fun way.

# About the Book

This book is aimed toward engaging children in a fun and rhyming learning style. It takes the reader through a typical day firefighters face while teaching important and potentially lifesaving lessons. The book starts with an overview of the fire station and the morning chores. Then it introduces the reader to equipment found on the fire truck and the firefighters' protective gear. After that, the reader goes on a journey with the fire department as the crew responds to an emergency and rescues a boy from a burning home. This is where children learn the importance of what to do if they find themselves in this situation, like calling 911, getting out and staying out, and not playing with matches. The book then finishes with the fire crew cleaning up the scene and returning to the station where they are always ready for the next emergency.

Printed in the United States
By Bookmasters